Ruth Miskin

Superphonics

Spelling

A systematic spelling programme

Contents

a div

D1424624

Introduction

Phonics is a highly effective way of teaching reading and spelling, based on the link between sounds and the way in which we write them down.

The aim of this book is to help children to become confident at spelling. When children are confident spellers, they can concentrate on what they write rather than worrying about spelling. Many children avoid using interesting and varied words in their writing because they cannot spell them.

This spelling book is unique in that it teaches children about the structure of English words, giving them strategies for spelling words correctly. Many English words are quite difficult to spell; *Superphonics Spelling* teaches the easy words first, gradually adding more difficult ones.

Section 1 covers the short vowel sounds (**a**, **e**, **i**, **o** and **u**), groups of consonants (e.g. **cl** and **ss**), and the simplest spelling for each long vowel sound (e.g. **ee** as in **sheep**).

Section 2 deals with alternative spellings for the long vowel sounds (e.g. **ea** as in **bead**, **e** as in **we** and **y** as in **happy**).

Section 3 looks at root words and word endings, and more complex spellings. The 'Useful words' unit at the back of the book gives practice in reading and spelling groups of words which are frequently needed but difficult to spell, such as contractions.

When to use the book

Any child can learn to spell using *Superphonics Spelling*. Ideally, the book should be used when your child has completed *Superphonics Books 1-5* (see p64), and can read the words in those books with confidence.

What you will need

The only extra materials you will need are a sharp pencil, a rubber and a notebook.

Terms used in the book

Sounds and letters

All words are made up of small units of sound.

Some sounds are represented by one letter (e.g. **a**, **b**).

Some sounds are represented by two letters (e.g. **sh**, **ee**).

Some sounds are represented by three or more letters (e.g. **igh**, **air**, **eigh**).

The word **c-a-t** contains three sounds.
The word **sh-o-p** contains three sounds.
The word **l-igh-t** contains three sounds.

When talking about sounds, say **a** as in **cat**, **b** as in **bed**, **c** as in **can**, etc.

When talking about letters, use the letter names (**ay**, **bee**, **see**, etc.)

The chart below analyses the sounds and letters used to build the kinds of word you will meet in this book. Try to familiarise yourself with it before starting to teach your child.

	Vowel sound	Letters used to write the vowel sound	Sounds*		Vowel sound	Letters used to write the vowel sound	Sounds*
tree	ee	ee	t-r-ee	down	ou	ow	d-ow-n
sea	ee	ea	s-ea	mouse	ou	ou	m-ou-se
she	ee	e	sh-e	shark	ar	ar	sh-ar-k
happy	ee	y	h-a-pp-y	grass	ar	a	g-r-a-ss
moon	oo	oo	m-oo-n	girl	ir	ir	g-ir-l
threw	oo	ew	th-r-ew	hurt	ir	ur	h-ur-t
blue	oo	ue	b-l-ue	her	ir	er	h-er
to	oo	o	t-o	boy	oi	oy	b-oy
play	ay	ay	p-l-ay	point	oi	oi	p-oi-n-t
came	ay	a-e	c-a-m e	chair	air	air	ch-air
paid	ay	ai	p-ai-d	share	air	are	sh-are
they	ay	ey	th-ey	bear	air	ear	b-ear
night	igh	igh	n-igh-t	there	air	ere	th-ere
time	igh	i-e	t-i-m e	fork	or	or	f-or-k
try	igh	y	t-r-y	crawl	or	aw	c-r-aw-l
pie	igh	ie	p-ie	ball	or	a	b-a-ll
throw	ow	ow	th-r-ow	door	or	oor	d-oor
hole	ow	o-e	h-o-l e	talk	or	al	t-al-k
boat	ow	oa	b-oa-t				
go	ow	o	g-o				

* Make each sound as short as possible. For example, say **b**, not **buh**.

Root words

A root word is the meaningful part of a word before any 'extras' are added. In the word **played**, the root word is **play**. In the word **turning**, the root word is **turn**.

Syllables

Words can be divided into beats, or syllables. The word **cat** has one syllable. The word **win/dow** has two syllables. The word **el/e/phant** has three syllables.

Key to print styles

Instructions for you to read to your child, and examples of answers, are presented in speech bubbles. The cat character gives helpful hints and extra information in his coloured speech bubbles. Groups of letters representing single sounds are separated by dashes.

e.g. **t-oo-th**

Words for your child to read are printed in large type on a white background. Letters representing the target sound are printed in green, silent letters in red and tricky words in blue. If more than one letter is used to represent a sound, these letters are underlined.

e.g. kn<u>ow</u> l<u>ow</u> the said

In Section 3, word endings are printed in bold type, and syllables are separated by forward slashes.

hop**ing**

win/dow

How to use the book

You will need only ten minutes each day for working on this book with your child. Start at the beginning, even if you know your child can spell most of the easier words. This will help him or her to get used to the **Superphonics** system without having to learn to spell new words at the same time. It will also make your child feel that spelling is easy!

Your child will need to revise each page frequently in order to become more and more familiar with the spellings. It's rather like practising the times tables to make him or her feel confident with maths. The test pages will show how much your child has progressed and indicate words that need revision.

Section 1

On pages 10-20, begin by reading the text at the top of the page (e.g. **What can you see in the tree?**) together. On all pages, read all the words, emphasising the target sound.

Step 1: Say the word.

Demonstrate reading each of the words in the panel at the top of the page, exaggerating the vowel sound (e.g. **day**). Ask your child to say the word in the same way.

This makes sure that he or she can hear all the sounds in the word, but most importantly the vowel sound. It is usually the vowel sound that is incorrectly spelled.

Step 2: Say the vowel sound.

Ask your child to say the vowel sound on its own (e.g. **ay**).

Step 3: Say all the sounds, counting them off on your fingers.

Ask your child to hold up one hand and count off the sounds on his or her fingers, saying the sound while touching each finger (e.g. **d-ay**).

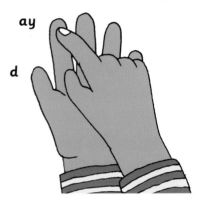

Step 4: Now trace the letter or letter group for each sound on the same fingers.

Still holding up the same number of fingers, your child should form the letter shapes on them, saying the letter names (e.g. **dee ay-wigh**). **If two or three letters are needed to make a sound, only one finger should be used for all those letters.**

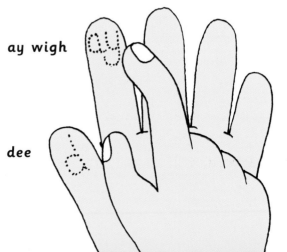

Step 5: Write the word. Say the word. Say the vowel sound. Underline the letter or letter group that makes that sound.

Ask your child to write the word, saying it clearly, and to check his or her spelling. If there are any errors, ask your child to tell you the sound that has been spelled incorrectly and to write the correct letters for that sound. (It is not necessary to rewrite the whole word.) Ask your child to underline the letter or letter group used to make the vowel sound.

Section 2

Follow the same steps as in Section 1.

In Section 2, your child will learn that vowel sounds can be represented in more than one way. For example, the **ay** sound can be spelled **ay** as in **day**, **a-e** as in **made**, **ai** as in **rain** and **ey** as in **they**. How will he or she know which of these groups of letters to use?

There are few hard and fast rules to learn; plenty of practice in reading and spelling the word are the key to success. If there is a choice of spellings (e.g. **weak** or **week**), put each word into a sentence to help your child to decide when to use each version.

Section 3

In this section, your child will learn to spell words with various endings (e.g. **raining**, **rained**). These endings are shown in the context of words that he or she will already be able to spell (e.g. **rain**). The same word endings (**ing**, **ed**, **s**, **y**, **er** and **est**) are repeated throughout the section so that your child will have plenty of opportunities to practise the spellings.

Step 1: Say the root word.

Ask your child to say the root word without the word ending (e.g. **rain**).

Step 2: Say the word ending.

Ask your child to say the word ending (e.g. **ing**).

The pronunciation of the ending may vary according to the root word it follows; the word ending **ed** can be pronounced **d** (as in **rained**), **id** (as in **needed**) or **t** (as in **hoped**). The word ending **s** can be pronounced **s** (as in **hopes**) or **z** (as in **knows**).

The second activity in Section 3 lets your child build upon what he or she has already learned about vowel sounds by applying it to longer words. Other vowel sounds are practised incidentally; for example, in the word **thirteen**, the letter pattern **ee** is practised as well as the target letter pattern, **ir**.

New knowledge is introduced, too. For example, in the word **peace**, your child will already know the **ea** spelling of the vowel sound but will now learn the **ce** spelling of the **s** sound.

He or she will also learn less common spellings of the target sound (e.g. **eigh** as in **weight**).

Step 1: Say the word syllable by syllable.

Ask your child to say the word syllable by syllable (e.g. **a/gree**). In some words (e.g. **Monday**), there is an irregular spelling

of a vowel sound (the **o** in **Mon**). For these words, encourage your child to say the word as he or she would expect it to sound, before pronouncing it correctly.

Step 2: Say the whole word.

Ask your child to say the whole word without a break (e.g. **agree**).

Step 3: Say the (**ee**) sound.

Ask your child to say the target vowel sound (e.g. **ee**).

Step 4: Now trace the letter group for the (**ee**) sound on your finger.

Ask your child to form the letters on his or her finger, saying the names of the letters (e.g. **ee ee**). *ee*

Step 5: Try writing the words from memory, three at a time. Underline all the letter groups in each word. Did you find any of the sounds difficult to spell? Circle that letter or letter group.

Ask your child to write the word, underline any group of letters which represents a single sound (e.g. **Tuesday**) and, if necessary, to circle the difficult letter or letter group.

Because your child has identified the difficult part of the word independently, and thought about it carefully, he or she will have a good chance of remembering the correct spelling.

Tricky words

Some words in the English language are not spelled as you would expect them to be from the way they sound. 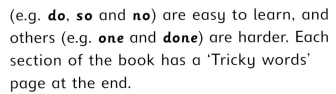 Some of these words (e.g. **do**, **so** and **no**) are easy to learn, and others (e.g. **one** and **done**) are harder. Each section of the book has a 'Tricky words' page at the end.

On this page, your child is asked to choose a group of words to practise spelling. These should be words that he or she finds more challenging than the others (e.g. **said**).

Next, your child is asked to identify the regular part(s) of the word (e.g. **s** and **d**). He or she is then asked to identify the 'tricky' part (e.g. **ai**).

Your child is then asked to repeat the letter names for the word without looking at the page (e.g. **ess ay-igh dee**). Clap out the rhythm as he or she says the letter names.

The next step is to practise writing the words while saying the letters in rhythm. Your child should then be asked to read the words back, deciding which are correctly spelled. It is important that he or she can recognise a word which 'just doesn't look right'.

At the bottom of the 'Tricky words' page there are some tips for remembering tricky spellings. However, if your child can invent his or her own techniques, he or she will learn even more effectively.

It is vital that you keep returning to these pages to practise spelling tricky words. They are all very common words that your child will need to use in his or her everyday writing.

Section 1: **Sounds and spellings**

Short words containing *a*, *e*, *i*, *o* or *u*

a	e	i	o	u
cat	bed	pig	dog	bug
cap	<u>th</u>en	dig	got	hug
can	ten	<u>ch</u>ip	cot	but

Reading

Step 1

Say the word.

Example: **cat**

Step 2

Say the vowel sound.

Example: **a**

(**a**, not **ay**)

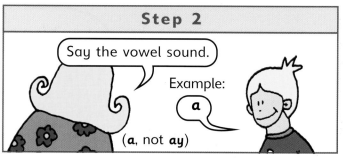

Step 3

Say all the sounds, counting them off on your fingers.

Example: **c-a-t**

(**c**, not **see**, etc.)

Step 4

Now trace the letter for each sound on the same fingers.

Writing

Step 5

Write the word.

Say the word. Say the vowel sound. Underline the letter that makes that sound.

Example: ca<u>t</u>

If you are wrong, have another go!

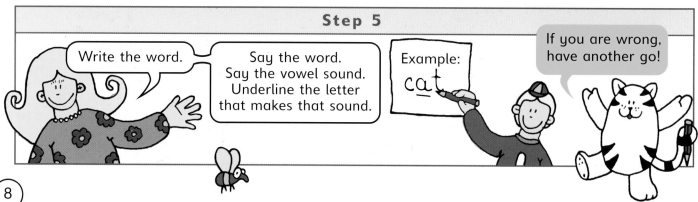

8

Words containing consonant blends or double letters

sh	ll	ss	ng	ck
fla<u>sh</u>	we<u>ll</u>	me<u>ss</u>	ki<u>ng</u>	so<u>ck</u>
cra<u>sh</u>	<u>sh</u>e<u>ll</u>	ki<u>ss</u>	ba<u>ng</u>	<u>th</u>i<u>ck</u>

Reading

Step 1

Say the word.

Example: flash

Step 2

Say the last sound.

Example: sh

Step 3

Say all the sounds, counting them off on your fingers.

Example: f-l-a-sh

(f, not eff, etc.)

Step 4

Now trace the letter or letter group (**sh**, **ll**, **ss**, **ng**, **ck** or **th**) for each sound on the same fingers.

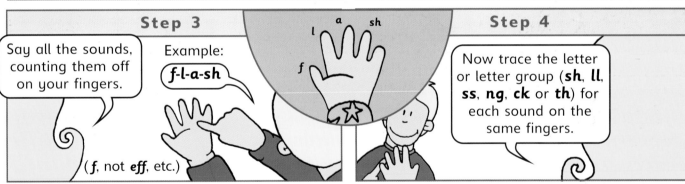

Writing

Step 5

Write the word.

Say the word. Say the last sound. Underline the letter group that makes that sound.

Example: fla<u>sh</u>

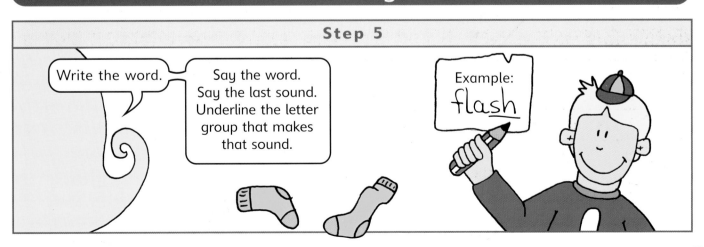

Words containing *ee*

ee What can you see in the tree?

see **tr<u>ee</u>** **n<u>ee</u>d** **<u>sh</u><u>ee</u>p**

<u>th</u>r<u>ee</u> **b<u>ee</u>n** **k<u>ee</u>p** **d<u>ee</u>p**

f<u>ee</u>l **sl<u>ee</u>p** **f<u>ee</u>d** **fr<u>ee</u>**

Say the question and all the words, emphasising the *ee* sound.

Reading

Step 1

Say the word.

Example:
see

Step 2

Say the vowel sound.

ee

Step 3

Say all the sounds, counting them off on your fingers.

Example:
s-ee

(**s**, not **ess**)

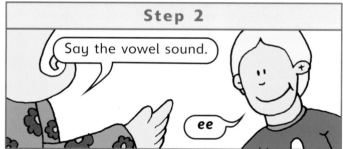

Step 4

Now trace the letter or letter group (**ee**, **sh** or **th**) for each sound on the same fingers.

Writing

Step 5

Write the word.

Say the word. Say the vowel sound. Underline the letter group that makes that sound.

Example:
s<u>ee</u>

Words containing oo (as in moon)

OO   Zoom to the moon!

moon	tooth	hoot
school	too	roof
boot	food	room

Say the sentence and all the words, emphasising the **oo** sound.

Reading

Step 1

Say the word.

Example: **moon**

Step 2

Say the vowel sound.

oo

Step 3

Say all the sounds, counting them off on your fingers.

Example: **m-oo-n**

(**m**, not **em**)

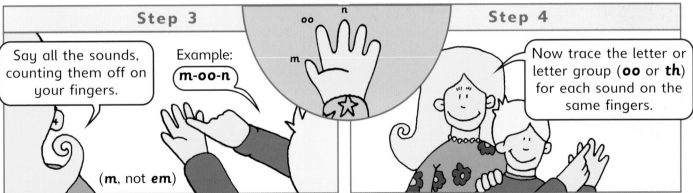

Step 4

Now trace the letter or letter group (**oo** or **th**) for each sound on the same fingers.

Writing

Step 5

Write the word.

Say the word. Say the vowel sound. Underline the letter group that makes that sound.

Example: moon

Words containing *ay*

ay May I play?

d<u>ay</u>	h<u>ay</u>	m<u>ay</u>	pl<u>ay</u>
p<u>ay</u>	l<u>ay</u>	w<u>ay</u>	cl<u>ay</u>
r<u>ay</u>	s<u>ay</u>	tr<u>ay</u>	st<u>ay</u>

Say the question and all the words, emphasising the **ay** sound.

Reading

ay usually comes at the end of a word.

Step 1

Say the word.

Example: **day**

Step 2

Say the vowel sound.

ay

Step 3

Say all the sounds, counting them off on your fingers.

Example: **d-ay**

(**d**, not **dee**)

ay

d

Step 4

Now trace the letter or letter group (**ay**) for each sound on the same fingers.

Writing

Step 5

Write the word.

Say the word. Say the vowel sound. Underline the letter group that makes that sound.

Example: d<u>ay</u>

Words containing *igh*

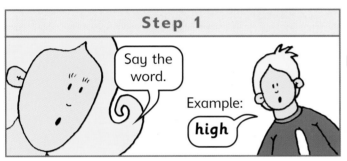

igh A bright light at night

h<u>igh</u>	l<u>igh</u>t	br<u>igh</u>t
fr<u>igh</u>t	n<u>igh</u>t	m<u>igh</u>t
s<u>igh</u>t	fl<u>igh</u>t	f<u>igh</u>t

Say the phrase and all the words, emphasising the **igh** sound.

Reading

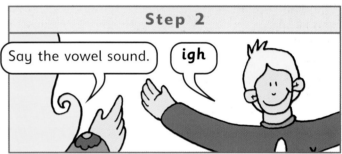

Step 1

Say the word.

Example: **high**

Step 2

Say the vowel sound.

igh

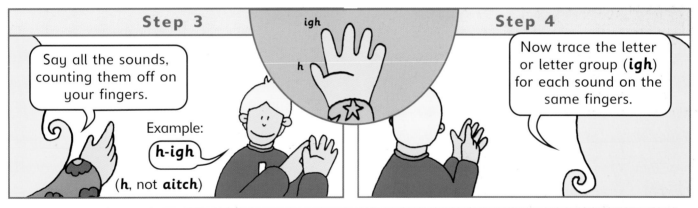

Step 3

Say all the sounds, counting them off on your fingers.

Example: **h-igh**

(**h**, not **aitch**)

igh

h

Step 4

Now trace the letter or letter group (**igh**) for each sound on the same fingers.

Writing

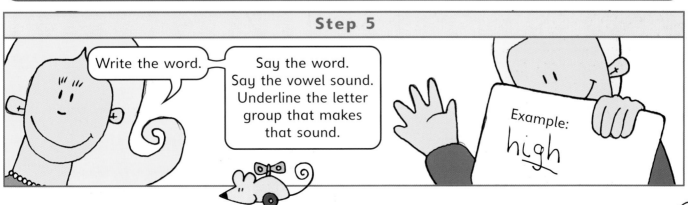

Step 5

Write the word.

Say the word. Say the vowel sound. Underline the letter group that makes that sound.

Example: high

Words containing **ow** (as in **snow**)

ow   Throw the snow!

sn<u>ow</u>	gr<u>ow</u>	kn<u>ow</u>
l<u>ow</u>	<u>sh</u><u>ow</u>	sl<u>ow</u>
<u>th</u>r<u>ow</u>	bl<u>ow</u>	fl<u>ow</u>

Say the sentence and all the words, emphasising the **ow** sound.

Reading

Step 1

Say the word.

Example: **snow**

Step 2

Say the vowel sound.

ow

Step 3

Say all the sounds, counting them off on your fingers.

Example: **s-n-ow**

(**s**, not **ess**, etc.)

Step 4

Now trace the letter or letter group (**ow**, **th** or **sh**) for each sound on the same fingers.

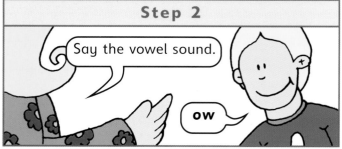

Writing

Step 5

Write the word.

Say the word. Say the vowel sound. Underline the letter group that makes that sound.

Example: sn<u>ow</u>

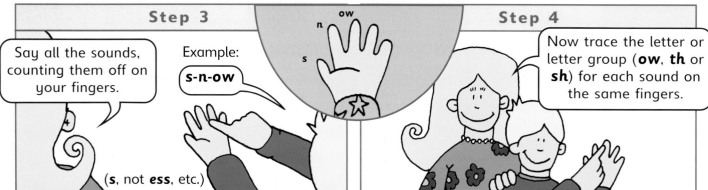

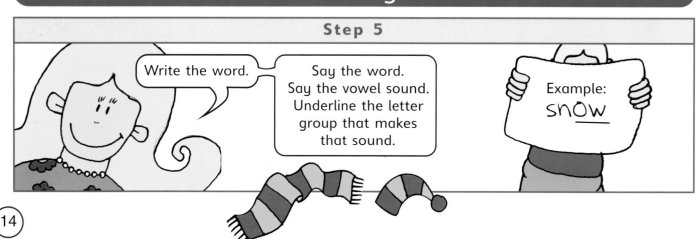

Words containing **ow** (as in **clown**)

OW   A clown in a crown

cl<u>ow</u>n   d<u>ow</u>n   br<u>ow</u>n

t<u>ow</u>n   n<u>ow</u>   fr<u>ow</u>n

cr<u>ow</u>n   g<u>ow</u>n   dr<u>ow</u>n

Say the phrase and all the words, emphasising the **ow** sound.

Reading

Step 1

Say the word.

Example: **clown**

Step 2

Say the vowel sound.

ow

Step 3

Say all the sounds, counting them off on your fingers.

Example: **c-l-ow-n**

(**c**, not **see**, etc.)

Step 4

Now trace the letter or letter group (**ow**) for each sound on the same fingers.

Writing

Step 5

Write the word.

Say the word. Say the vowel sound. Underline the letter group that makes that sound.

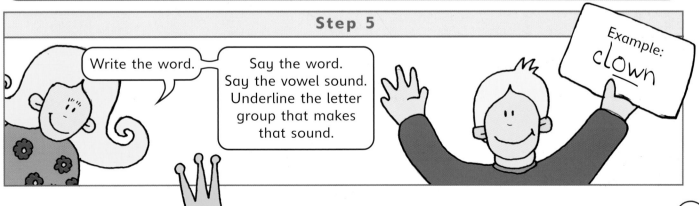

Example: cl<u>ow</u>n

15

Words containing **ar**

ar Start the car.

card farm dark bar
start car hard sharp
far arm park shark

Say the sentence and all the words, emphasising the **ar** sound.

Reading

Step 1

Say the word.

Example:

card

Step 2

Say the vowel sound.

ar

Step 3

Say all the sounds, counting them off on your fingers.

Example:

c-ar-d

(**c**, not **see**, etc.)

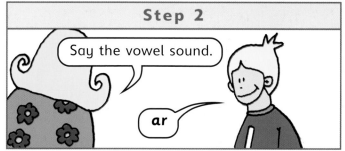

Step 4

Now trace the letter or letter group (**ar** or **sh**) for each sound on the same fingers.

Writing

Step 5

Write the word.

Say the word. Say the vowel sound. Underline the letter group that makes that sound.

Example:
card

Words containing *ir*

ir   The third bird

girl b<u>ir</u>d st<u>ir</u> <u>sh</u>ir<u>t</u>

<u>th</u>ird d<u>ir</u>t sk<u>ir</u>t f<u>ir</u>st

s<u>qu</u>ir<u>t</u> f<u>ir</u> <u>th</u>irst f<u>ir</u>m

Say the phrase and all the words, emphasising the **ir** sound.

Reading

Step 1

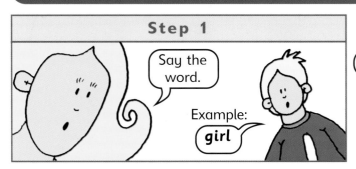

Say the word.

Example: **girl**

Step 2

Say the vowel sound.

ir

Step 3

Say all the sounds, counting them off on your fingers.

Example: **g-ir-l**

(**g**, not **jee**, etc.)

Step 4

Now trace the letter or letter group (**ir**, **sh**, **qu** or **th**) for each sound on the same fingers.

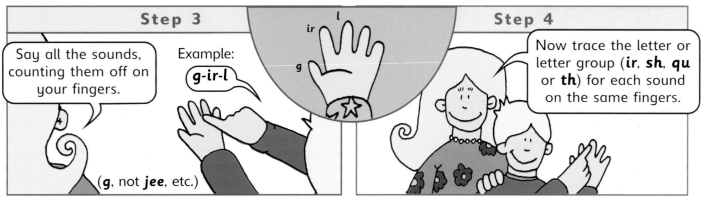

Writing

Step 5

Write the word.

Say the word. Say the vowel sound. Underline the letter group that makes that sound.

Example: girl

Words containing **oy**

oy   A toy for a boy

b<u>oy</u>   j<u>oy</u>

enj<u>oy</u>   t<u>oy</u>

a<u>nn</u><u>oy</u>

Say the phrase and all the words, emphasising the **oy** sound.

Reading

Step 1

Say the word.

Example:
boy

Step 2

Say the vowel sound.

oy

Step 3

Say all the sounds, counting them off on your fingers.

Example:
b-oy

(**b**, not **bee**)

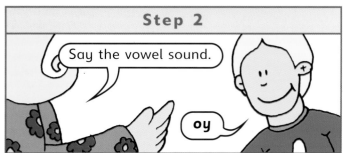

Step 4

Now trace the letter or letter group (**oy** or **nn**) for each sound on the same fingers.

Writing

Step 5

Write the word.

Say the word. Say the vowel sound. Underline the letter group that makes that sound.

Example:
b<u>oy</u>

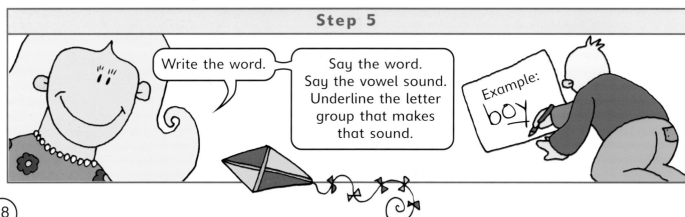

Words containing *air*

air   That's not fair!

ch<u>air</u>   <u>air</u>   h<u>air</u>
f<u>air</u>   p<u>air</u>   l<u>air</u>
st<u>air</u>

Say the sentence and all the words, emphasising the **air** sound.

Reading

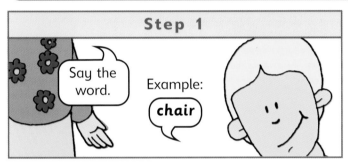

Step 1

Say the word.

Example: **chair**

Step 2

Say the vowel sound.

air

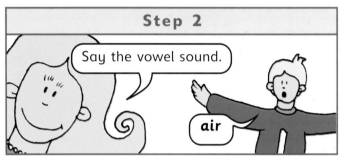

Step 3

Say all the sounds, counting them off on your fingers.

Example: **ch-air**

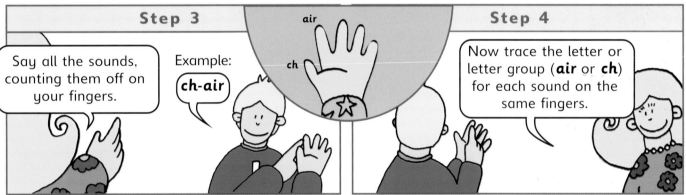

Step 4

Now trace the letter or letter group (**air** or **ch**) for each sound on the same fingers.

Writing

Step 5

Write the word.

Say the word. Say the vowel sound. Underline the letter group that makes that sound.

Example: ch<u>air</u>

Words containing **or**

or A horse in a storm

f**or**k	b**or**n	sp**or**t	s**or**t
f**or**	**sh**ort	t**or**n	w**or**n
st**or**m	h**or**se	**sh**ort	

Say the phrase and all the words, emphasising the **or** sound.

Reading

Step 1

Say the word.

Example:
fork

Step 2

Say the vowel sound.

or

Step 3

Say all the sounds, counting them off on your fingers.

Example:
f-or-k

(**f**, not **eff**, etc.)

Step 4

Now trace the letter or letter group (**or**, **sh** or **se**) for each sound on the same fingers.

Writing

Step 5

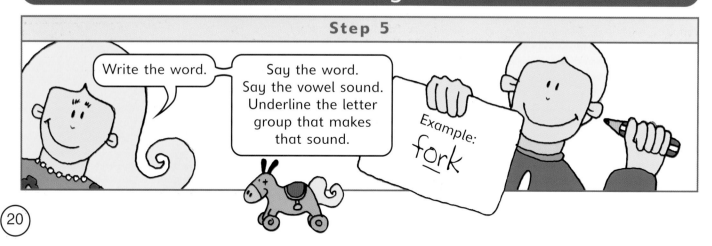

Write the word.

Say the word. Say the vowel sound. Underline the letter group that makes that sound.

Example:
f**or**k

Tricky words

said   was   come   have

the   they   some   live

I   when   give

Choose three words that you would like to practise spelling today.

Example: **said**

Point to the easy parts.

Example: **s d**

Point to the tricky part.

Example: **ai**

Say all the letter names in the whole word over and over again, without looking at the word.

Cover the page. Now I'm going to say your three words, one at a time. Write each word down.

Example: *said*

Are there any words you are not sure about? Circle the tricky part of the word, and then write the word again.

Here are some tips for remembering some of these spellings.

some come	when
Say each of these as two separate words: **so me co me**	Look for the **hen** in **when**!

man	crash	play	stair
ship	clock	born	school
dog	sing	girl	fight
hut	dress	house	blow
pen		start	three
		toy	

Read each of these 20 words aloud, and ask your child to write it down.

At the end of the test, praise him or her for working so hard and spelling so many words correctly.

Circle any words that are wrongly spelled.

Important!

If the vowel part of a word (**a**, **e**, **i**, **o** or **u**; **ee**, **oo**, **ay**, **igh** or **ow**; **ou**, **ar**, **ir**, **oy**, **air** or **or**) is misspelled, your child needs to revisit the relevant page in Section 1 before starting Section 2.

Section 2: **More spellings**

ee	ea	e	y
s<u>ee</u>	sp<u>ea</u>k	he	happ<u>y</u>
tr<u>ee</u>	w<u>ea</u>k	me	ugl<u>y</u>
n<u>ee</u>d	r<u>ea</u>d	<u>sh</u>e	onl<u>y</u>
sl<u>ee</u>p	<u>ea</u><u>ch</u>	be	bod<u>y</u>

Reading

Step 1

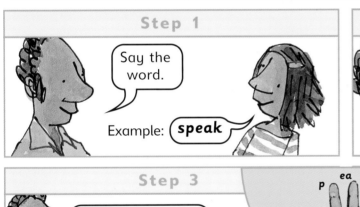

Say the word.

Example: **speak**

Step 2

Say the vowel sound.

Example: **ea**

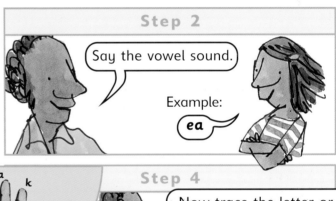

Step 3

Say all the sounds, counting them off on your fingers.

Example: **s-p-ea-k**

(**s**, not **ess**, etc.)

Step 4

Now trace the letter or letter group (**ee**, **ea**, **ch**, **sh** or **pp**) for each sound on the same fingers.

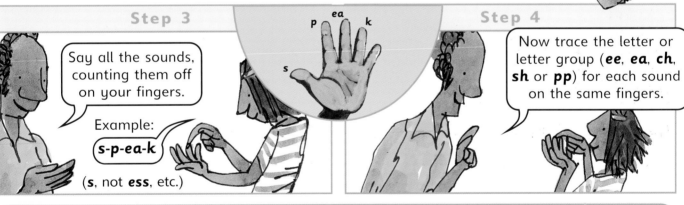

Writing

Step 5

Write the word.

Say the word. Say the vowel sound. Underline the letter or letter group that makes that sound.

Example: sp<u>ea</u>k

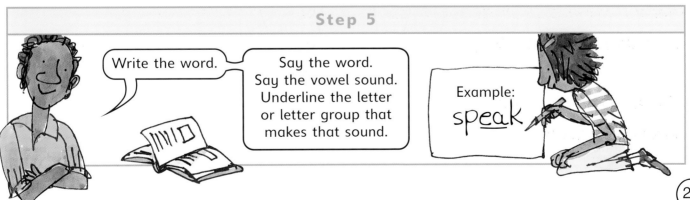

Words containing oo, ew, ue or o

oo	ew	ue	o
t**oo**th	bl**ew**	bl**ue**	t**o**
sch**oo**l	**ch**ew	tr**ue**	tw**o**
r**oo**m	n**ew**	cl**ue**	d**o**
s**oo**n	f**ew**		wh**o**

Look for two pairs of words that sound the same. What do they mean?

Reading

Step 1

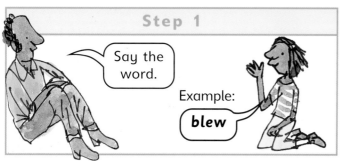

Say the word.

Example:

blew

Step 2

Say the vowel sound.

ew

Step 3

Say all the sounds, counting them off on your fingers.

Example:

b-l-ew

(**b**, not **bee**, etc.)

Step 4

Now trace the letter or letter group (**ew**, **oo**, **ue**, **ch** or **th**) for each sound on the same fingers.

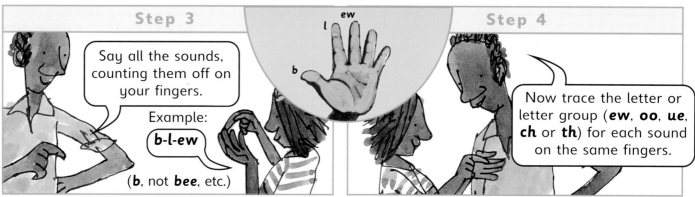

Writing

Step 5

Write the word.

Say the word. Say the vowel sound. Underline the letter or letter group that makes that sound.

Example:

bl**ew**

Words containing ay, a–e, ai or ey

ay	a–e	ai	ey
d<u>ay</u>	m<u>a</u>d<u>e</u>	r<u>ai</u>n	th<u>ey</u>
pl<u>ay</u>	m<u>a</u>k<u>e</u>	tr<u>ai</u>n	
w<u>ay</u>	c<u>a</u>m<u>e</u>	m<u>ai</u>n	
s<u>ay</u>	g<u>a</u>m<u>e</u>	pl<u>ai</u>n	

a–e
These two letters make one vowel sound.

They look as if they are holding hands.

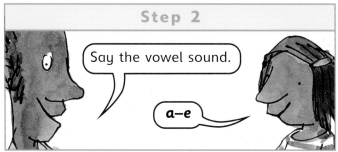

Reading

Step 1

Say the word.

Example: **made**

Step 2

Say the vowel sound.

a–e

Step 3

Say all the sounds, counting them off on your fingers.

Example: m-a-d e

(**m**, not **em**, etc.)

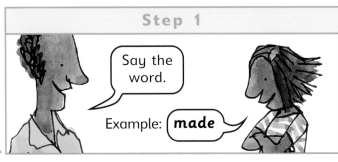

Step 4

Now trace the letter or letter group (**ay**, **ai**, **a–e**, **ey** or **th**) for each sound on the same fingers.

Writing

Step 5

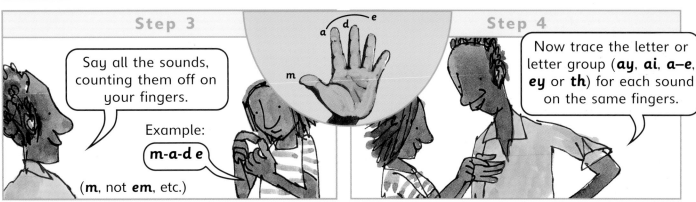

Write the word.

Say the word. Say the vowel sound. Underline the letter group that makes that sound.

Example:

m<u>a</u>d<u>e</u>

Words containing *igh*, *i–e*, *y* or *ie*

igh	i–e	y	ie
high	time	by	lie
night	mine	my	die
light	shine	try	pie
sigh	write	why	tie

i–e
These two letters make one vowel sound.

They look as if they are holding hands.

Reading

Step 1

Say the word.

Example: **time**

Step 2

Say the vowel sound.

i–e

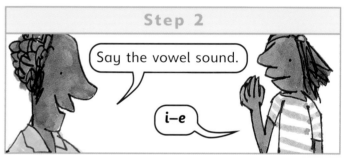

Step 3

Say all the sounds, counting them off on your fingers.

Example:
t-i-m e

(**t**, not **tee**, etc.)

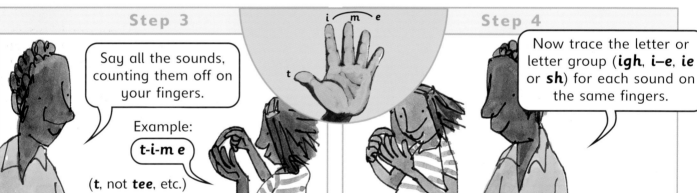

Step 4

Now trace the letter or letter group (**igh**, **i–e**, **ie** or **sh**) for each sound on the same fingers.

Writing

Step 5

Write the word.

Say the word. Say the vowel sound. Underline the letter or letter group that makes that sound.

Example:
time

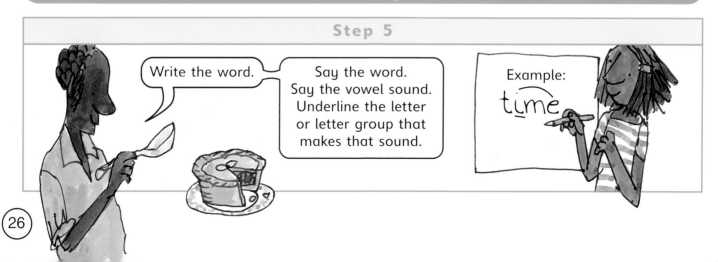

Words containing ow, o–e, oa or o

ow	o–e	oa	o
kn<u>ow</u>	hope	b<u>oa</u>t	s<u>o</u>
l<u>ow</u>	joke	fl<u>oa</u>t	g<u>o</u>
<u>th</u>r<u>ow</u>	<u>ph</u>one	c<u>oa</u>t	n<u>o</u>
bl<u>ow</u>	hole	<u>th</u>r<u>oa</u>t	

o–e
These two letters make one vowel sound.

They look as if they are holding hands.

Reading

Step 1

Say the word.

Example: **hope**

Step 2

Say the vowel sound.

o–e

Step 3

Say all the sounds, counting them off on your fingers.

Example: **h-o-p e**

(**h**, not **aitch**, etc.)

Step 4

Now trace the letter or letter group (**ow**, **o–e**, **oa**, **th** or **ph**) for each sound on the same fingers.

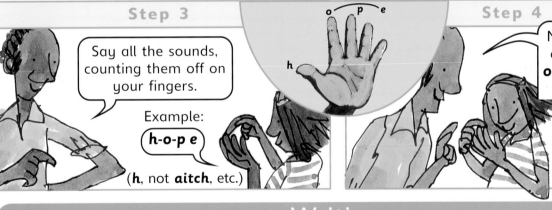

Writing

Step 5

Write the word.

Say the word. Say the vowel sound. Underline the letter or letter group that makes that sound.

Example: hope

Words containing ou or ow

ou		ow	
sh<u>ou</u>t	r<u>ou</u>nd	br<u>ow</u>n	d<u>ow</u>n
c<u>ou</u>nt	f<u>ou</u>nd	c<u>ow</u>	t<u>ow</u>n
l<u>ou</u>d	m<u>ou</u>se	n<u>ow</u>	fr<u>ow</u>n
h<u>ou</u>se	ab<u>ou</u>t	h<u>ow</u>	

In these words, **ow** makes the same sound as **ou**.

Reading

Step 1

Say the word.

Example: **shout**

Step 2

Say the vowel sound.

ou

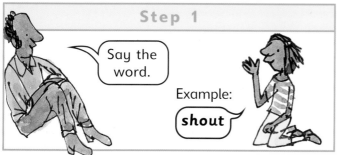

Step 3

Say all the sounds, counting them off on your fingers.

Example: **sh-ou-t**

(**t**, not **tee**)

Step 4

Now trace the letter or letter group (**ou**, **ow**, **sh** or **se**) for each sound on the same fingers.

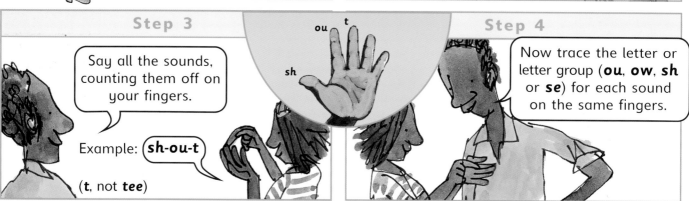

Writing

Step 5

Write the word.

Say the word. Say the vowel sound. Underline the letter group that makes that sound.

Example: sh<u>ou</u>t

28

Words containing *ar* or *a*

ar		*a* (Southern accents only)	
c<u>ar</u>d	f<u>ar</u>m	gr<u>ass</u>	f<u>a</u>st
b<u>ar</u>	st<u>ar</u>t	p<u>ass</u>	l<u>a</u>st
f<u>ar</u>	<u>sh</u><u>ar</u>p	b<u>a</u><u>th</u>	p<u>a</u>st
<u>ar</u>m	m<u>ar</u><u>ch</u>	p<u>a</u><u>th</u>	c<u>a</u>st

Reading

Step 1

Say the word.

Example: **card**

Step 2

Say the vowel sound.

ar

Step 3

Say all the sounds, counting them off on your fingers.

Example: **c-ar-d**

(**c**, not **see**, etc.)

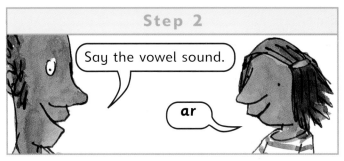

Step 4

Now trace the letter or letter group (**ar**, **ch**, **sh**, **th** or **ss**) for each sound on the same fingers.

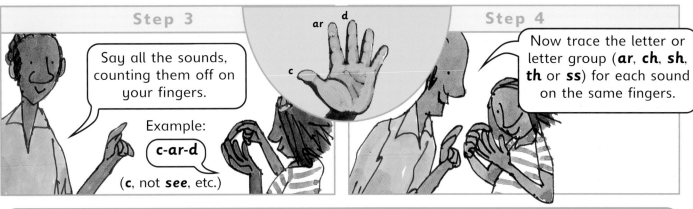

Writing

Step 5

Write the word.

Say the word. Say the vowel sound. Underline the letter or letter group that makes that sound.

Example: c<u>ar</u>d

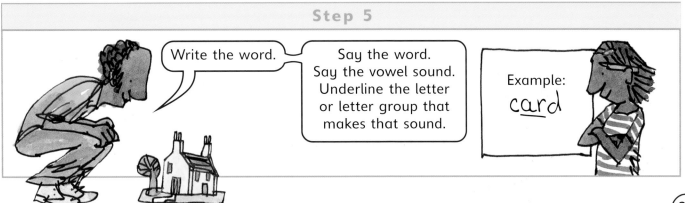

Words containing *ir*, *ur* or *er*

ir	ur	er
g<u>ir</u>l	h<u>ur</u>t	h<u>er</u>
<u>sh</u><u>ir</u>t	t<u>ur</u>n	nev<u>er</u>
sk<u>ir</u>t	n<u>ur</u><u>se</u>	
d<u>ir</u>t	p<u>ur</u><u>se</u>	

Reading

Step 1

Say the word.

Example: (**hurt**)

Step 2

Say the vowel sound.

(**ur**)

Step 3

Say all the sounds, counting them off on your fingers.

Example:

(**h-ur-t**)

(**h**, not **aitch**, etc.)

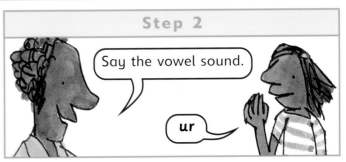

Step 4

Now trace the letter or letter group (**ir**, **ur**, **er**, **sh** or **se**) for each sound on the same fingers.

Writing

Step 5

Write the word.

Say the word. Say the vowel sound. Underline the letter group that makes that sound.

Example:

h<u>ur</u>t

Words containing oy or oi

oy		oi	
b<u>oy</u>	enj<u>oy</u>	sp<u>oi</u>l	v<u>oi</u>ce
t<u>oy</u>	ann<u>oy</u>	b<u>oi</u>l	p<u>oi</u>nt
j<u>oy</u>		<u>ch</u><u>oi</u>ce	j<u>oi</u>n
		n<u>oi</u>se	c<u>oi</u>n

Reading

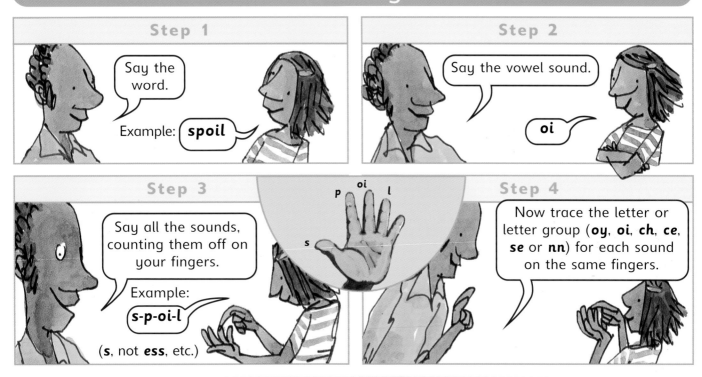

Step 1

Say the word.

Example: **spoil**

Step 2

Say the vowel sound.

oi

Step 3

Say all the sounds, counting them off on your fingers.

Example:

s-p-oi-l

(**s**, not **ess**, etc.)

p   oi   l

s

Step 4

Now trace the letter or letter group (**oy**, **oi**, **ch**, **ce**, **se** or **nn**) for each sound on the same fingers.

Writing

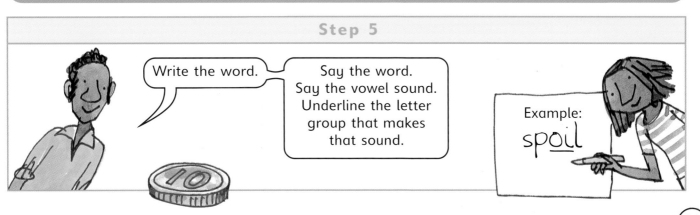

Step 5

Write the word.

Say the word. Say the vowel sound. Underline the letter group that makes that sound.

Example: sp<u>oi</u>l

Words containing *air*, *are*, *ear* or *ere*

air	are	ear	ere
ch<u>air</u>	c<u>are</u>	b<u>ear</u>	th<u>ere</u>
h<u>air</u>	st<u>are</u>	w<u>ear</u>	wh<u>ere</u>
p<u>air</u>	sh<u>are</u>	p<u>ear</u>	
st<u>air</u>	r<u>are</u>		

Look for two pairs of words that sound the same. What do they mean?

Reading

Step 1

Say the word.

Example: **care**

Step 2

Say the vowel sound.

are

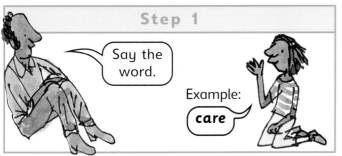

Step 3

Say all the sounds, counting them off on your fingers.

Example: **c-are**

(**c**, not **see**)

Step 4

Now trace the letter or letter group (**air**, **are**, **ear**, **ere**, **ch**, **sh**, **wh** or **th**) for each sound on the same fingers.

Writing

Step 5

Write the word.

Say the word. Say the vowel sound. Underline the letter group that makes that sound.

Example: c<u>are</u>

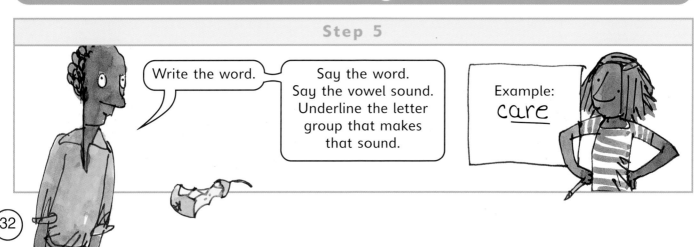

Words containing or, aw, a, oor or al

or	aw	a	oor	al
f<u>or</u>k	dr<u>aw</u>	b<u>all</u>	p<u>oor</u>	w<u>al</u>k
f<u>or</u>	j<u>aw</u>	f<u>all</u>	d<u>oor</u>	t<u>al</u>k
st<u>or</u>m	p<u>aw</u>	t<u>all</u>	fl<u>oor</u>	
h<u>or</u><u>se</u>	cr<u>aw</u>l	w<u>all</u>		

What a lot of spellings for one sound!

Reading

Step 1

Say the word.

Example: **draw**

Step 2

Say the vowel sound.

aw

Step 3

Say all the sounds, counting them off on your fingers.

Example: **d-r-aw**

(**d**, not **dee**, etc.)

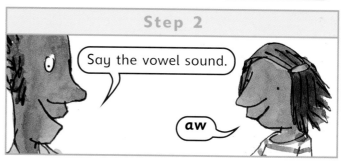

Step 4

Now trace the letter or letter group (**or**, **aw**, **oor**, **al**, **se** or **ll**) for each sound on the same fingers.

Writing

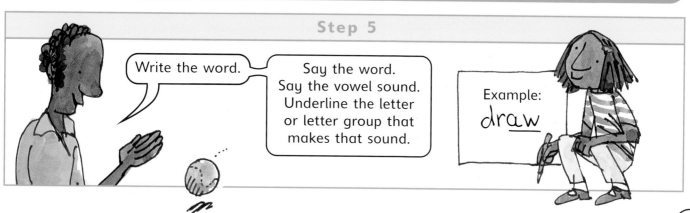

Step 5

Write the word.

Say the word. Say the vowel sound. Underline the letter or letter group that makes that sound.

Example: dr<u>aw</u>

33

Tricky words

one	love	what	who	were	buy
done	move	where	which	because	water
gone	your	why	when	won	only
once	four	could	there	son	people
does	more	would	their		friend
goes		should			

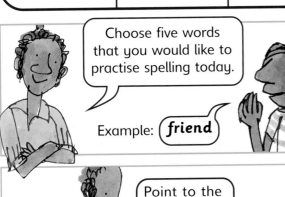

Choose five words that you would like to practise spelling today.

Example: friend

Point to the easy parts.

Example: **f r n d**

Point to the tricky part.

Example: **ie**

Say all the letter names in the whole word over and over again, without looking at the word.

Cover the page. Now I'm going to say your five words, one at a time. Write each word down.

Example: friend

Are there any words you are not sure about? Circle the tricky part of the word, and then write the word again.

Here are some tips for remembering some of these spellings.

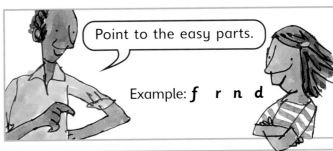

once
This word means **one** time; just put a **c** into **one**.

what where why who which when
All these question words begin with **wh**.

need each he happy	room grew true to	made day train they	night time try pie	throw hope coat so	house down
start fast	hurt bird her	boy noise	chair share there wear	horse draw door talk ball	

Read each of these 38 words aloud, and ask your child to write it down.

At the end of the test, praise him or her for working so hard and spelling so many words correctly.

Circle any words that are wrongly spelled.

Important!

If the vowel part of a word (**ee, ea, e** or **y**; **oo, ew, ue** or **o**; **ay, a-e, ai** or **ey**; **igh, i-e, y** or **ie**; **ow, o-e, oa** or **o**; **ou** or **ow**; **ar** or **a**; **ir, ur** or **er**; **oy** or **oi**; **air, are, ear** or **ere**; **or, aw, a, oor** or **al**) is misspelled, your child needs to revisit the relevant page in Section 2 before starting Section 3.

Words containing oo, ew, ue, o or ough

Before we start this page, let's look back at page 24 ...

Now let's look at some of those words – with endings added to them.

ing	ed	s	er	est
chew**ing**	chew**ed**	chew**s**	soon**er**	soon**est**
		room**s**	few**er**	few**est**
			new**er**	new**est**

Reading

Step 1

Say the root word.

Example: **chew**

Step 2

Say the word ending.

Example: **d**

Here are some longer words which have the **oo** sound in them.

In the word **through**, this vowel sound is spelled **ough**.

ew	ue	ough
neph/<u>ew</u>	res/c<u>ue</u>	th<u>rough</u>
f<u>ew</u>/<u>er</u>	con/tin/<u>ue</u>	
	<u>ar</u>/g<u>ue</u>	

Reading

Step 1

Say the word syllable by syllable.

Example: **neph/ew**

Step 2

Say the whole word.

Example: **nephew**

Step 3

Say the **ew** sound.

ew

Step 4

Now trace the letter group for the **ew** sound on your finger.

Writing

Step 5

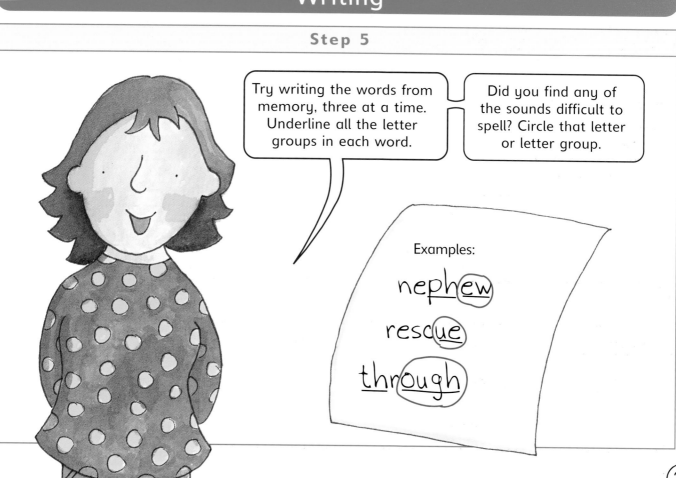

Try writing the words from memory, three at a time. Underline all the letter groups in each word.

Did you find any of the sounds difficult to spell? Circle that letter or letter group.

Examples:

nephew

rescue

through

Words containing *ay*, *a–e*, *ai*, *ey* or *eigh*

Before we start this page, let's look back at page 25 ...

Now let's look at some of those words – with endings added to them.

ing	ed	s	y	er	est
rain**ing**	rain**ed**	say**s**	rain**y**	plain**er**	plain**est**
play**ing**	play**ed**	game**s**			
say**ing**	train**ed**	train**s**			

Reading

The word ending **ed** can be pronounced **d**, **id** or **t**.

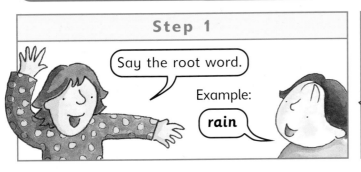

Step 1

Say the root word.

Example: **rain**

Step 2

Say the word ending.

Example: **d**

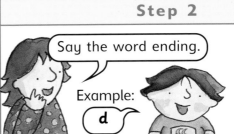

Here are some longer words which have the **ay** sound in them.

In a few words, this vowel sound is spelled **eigh**.

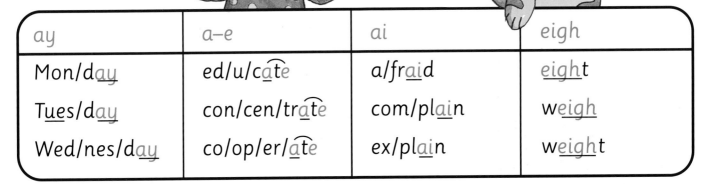

ay	a–e	ai	eigh
Mon/d<u>ay</u>	ed/u/c<u>a</u>te	a/fr<u>ai</u>d	<u>eigh</u>t
T<u>ue</u>s/d<u>ay</u>	con/cen/tr<u>a</u>te	com/pl<u>ai</u>n	w<u>eigh</u>
Wed/nes/d<u>ay</u>	co/op/er/<u>a</u>te	ex/pl<u>ai</u>n	w<u>eigh</u>t

Reading

Step 1

Say the word syllable by syllable. Say it as you would expect it to sound. Then say it correctly.

Example: **Mon/day**

Step 2

Say the whole word.

Example: **Monday**

Step 3

Say the **ay** sound.

ay

Step 4

Now trace the letter group for the **ay** sound on your finger.

Writing

Step 5

Try writing the words from memory, three at a time. Underline all the letter groups in each word.

Did you find any of the sounds difficult to spell? Circle that letter or letter group.

Examples:

Tuesday

concentrate

eight

Words containing *igh*, *i–e*, *y* or *ie*

Before we start this page, let's look back at page 26 ...

Now let's look at some of those words – with endings added to them.

ing	ed	s	y	er ier	est iest
light**ing**	sigh**ed**	shine**s**	shin**y**	shin**ier**	shin**iest**
tim**ing**	tim**ed**	time**s**		light**er**	light**est**
		light**s**		high**er**	high**est**

Reading

The **y** changes to **i** to make **shinier** and **shiniest**.

Step 1	Step 2

Say the root word.

shine

Say the word ending.

Example: **y**

Here are some longer words which have the **igh** sound in them.

igh	i–e	y
to/n**igh**t	de/c**i**de	re/pl**y**
de/l**igh**t	be/s**i**de	mult/i/pl**y**
	croc/o/d**i**le	sat/is/f**y**

Reading

Step 1

Say the word syllable by syllable.

Example: **de/cide**

Step 2

Say the whole word.

decide

Step 3

Say the **i–e** sound.

i–e

Step 4

Now trace the letter group for the **i–e** sound on your finger.

Writing

Step 5

Try writing the words from memory, three at a time. Underline all the letter groups in each word.

Did you find any of the sounds difficult to spell? Circle that letter or letter group.

Examples:

tonight

multiply

decide

Words containing ow, o–e, oa, o or ough

Before we start this page, let's look back at page 27 ...

Now let's look at some of those words – with endings added to them.

You can't have an **e** with an **ing**.

ing	ed	s	er	est
hop**ing**	hop**ed**	know**s**	low**er**	low**est**
jok**ing**	jok**ed**	hole**s**		
phon**ing**	phon**ed**	float**s**		

Reading

Step 1	Step 2
 Say the root word. Example: **hope**	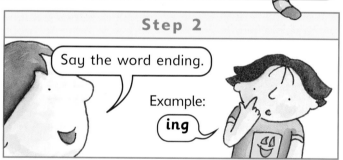 Say the word ending. Example: **ing**

Here are some longer words which have the **ow** sound in them.

In a few words, this vowel sound is spelled **ough**.

ow	o–e	ough
borr/<u>ow</u>	a/l<u>o</u>n̂e	<u>th</u><u>ough</u>
win/d<u>ow</u>	tel/e/p<u>h</u>ône	al/<u>th</u><u>ough</u>
to/mo<u>rr</u>/<u>ow</u>	supp/<u>o</u>ŝe	

Reading

Step 1

Say the word syllable by syllable.

Example:
borr/ow

Step 2

Say the whole word.

Example:
borrow

Step 3

Say the **ow** sound.

ow

Step 4

Now trace the letter group for the **ow** sound on your finger.

Writing

Step 5

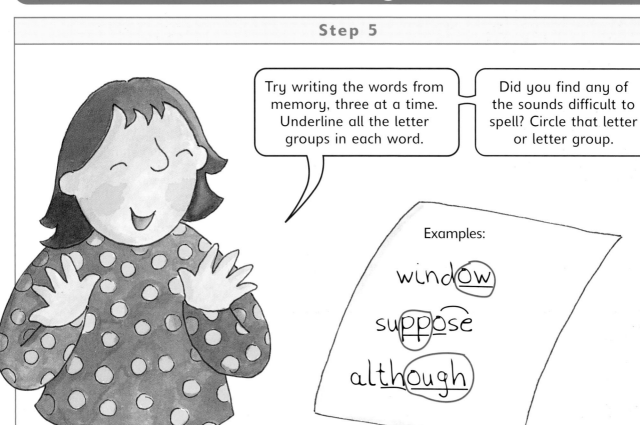

Try writing the words from memory, three at a time. Underline all the letter groups in each word.

Did you find any of the sounds difficult to spell? Circle that letter or letter group.

Examples:

window

suppose

although

Words containing **ou** or **ow**

Before we start this page, let's look back at page 28 …

Now let's look at some of those words – with endings added to them.

ing	ed	s	ly	er	est
shout**ing**	shout**ed**	cow**s**	loud**ly**	loud**er**	loud**est**
count**ing**	count**ed**	town**s**		round**er**	round**est**
		house**s**		brown**er**	brown**est**

The word **houses** is pronounced **houziz**.

Reading

Step 1

Say the root word.

Example:

house

Step 2

Say the word ending.

Example:

s

The word **loudly** is pronounced **loudlee**.

Here are some longer words which have the **ou** sound in them.

ow	ou
fl<u>ow</u>/<u>er</u> p<u>ow</u>/d<u>er</u> sh<u>ow</u>/<u>er</u>	bl<u>ou</u>se tr<u>ou</u>/s<u>er</u>s und<u>er</u>/gr<u>ou</u>nd
t<u>ow</u>/<u>er</u>	a/m<u>ou</u>nt m<u>ou</u>nt/<u>ai</u>n wi<u>th</u>/<u>ou</u>t
d<u>ow</u>n/st<u>ai</u>rs	a/r<u>ou</u>nd c<u>ou</u>nt/<u>er</u> r<u>ou</u>nd/a/b<u>ou</u>t

Reading

Step 1

Say the word syllable by syllable.

Example: flow/er

Step 2

Say the whole word.

Example: flower

Step 3

Say the **ow** sound.

ow

Step 4

Now trace the letter group for the **ow** sound on your finger.

Writing

Step 5

Try writing the words from memory, three at a time. Underline all the letter groups in each word.

Did you find any of the sounds difficult to spell? Circle that letter or letter group.

Examples:

blouse

mountain

trousers

Words containing *ar* or *a*

Before we start this page, let's look back at page 29 ...

Now let's look at some of those words – with endings added to them.

ing	ed	es	ly	er	est
march**ing**	march**ed**	march**es**	sharp**ly**	sharp**er**	sharp**est**
pass**ing**	pass**ed**	pass**es**	last**ly**	fast**er**	fast**est**
start**ing**	start**ed**	grass**es**			

Reading

Step 1	Step 2

Say the root word.

Example: **march**

Say the word ending.

The word ending **ed** can be pronounced **d**, **id** or **t**.

Example: **d**

Here are some longer words which have the **ar** sound in them.

ar	a (Southern accents only)
<u>ar</u>/gu/ment <u>ar</u>/tist re/m<u>ar</u>k	gr<u>aph</u> <u>ph</u>o/to/gr<u>aph</u> b<u>ath</u>/r<u>oo</u>m
de/p<u>ar</u>t/ment h<u>ar</u>m/le<u>ss</u>	tra<u>nce</u> da<u>nce</u> <u>ch</u>a<u>nce</u>

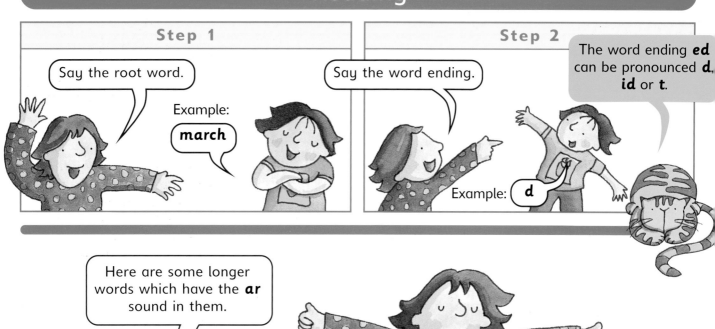

Reading

Step 1

Say the word syllable by syllable.

Example:

ar/gu/ment

Step 2

Say the whole word.

Example:

argument

Step 3

Say the **ar** sound.

ar

Step 4

Now trace the letter group for the **ar** sound on your finger.

Writing

Step 5

Try writing the words from memory, three at a time. Underline all the letter groups in each word.

Did you find any of the sounds difficult to spell? Circle that letter or letter group.

Examples:

argument

dance

graph

Words containing **ir**, **ur** or **er**

Before we start this page, let's look back at page 30 …

Now let's look at some of those words – with endings added to them.

ing	ed	s	y	ier	est
turn**ing**	turn**ed**	turn**s**	dirt**y**	dirt**ier**	dirt**iest**
nurs**ing**	nurs**ed**	nurse**s**			
hurt**ing**		hurt**s**			

Reading

Step 1	Step 2
	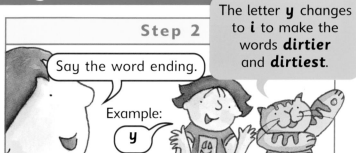

Say the root word.

Example: **dirt**

Say the word ending.

Example: **y**

The letter **y** changes to **i** to make the words **dirtier** and **dirtiest**.

Here are some longer words which have the **ir** sound in them.

ir	ur	er
b<u>ir</u>th/d<u>ay</u> th<u>ir</u>/ty	c<u>ur</u>/t<u>ai</u>n p<u>ur</u>/p<u>le</u>	butt/<u>er</u>
th<u>ir</u>/t<u>ee</u>n	Th<u>ur</u>s/d<u>ay</u>	su<u>mm</u>/<u>er</u>

Reading

Step 1

Say the word syllable by syllable.

Example:

birth/day

Step 2

Say the whole word.

Example:

birthday

Step 3

Say the **ir** sound.

ir

Step 4

Now trace the letter group for the **ir** sound on your finger.

Writing

Step 5

Try writing the words from memory, three at a time. Underline all the letter groups in each word.

Did you find any of the sounds difficult to spell? Circle that letter or letter group.

Examples:

thirty

curtain

butter

Words containing **oy** or **oi**

Before we start this page, let's look back at page 31 ...

Now let's look at some of those words – with endings added to them.

ing	ed	s	y	ier	est
enjoy**ing**	enjoy**ed**	enjoy**s**	nois**y**	nois**ier**	nois**iest**
spoil**ing**	spoil**ed**	spoil**s**			
point**ing**	point**ed**	point**s**			

Reading

The word **noisy** is pronounced **noizy**.

The letter **y** changes to **i** to make the words **noisier** and **noisiest.**

Step 1

Say the root word.

Example: **noisy**

Step 2

Say the word ending.

Example: **ier**

Here are some longer words which have the **oy** sound in them.

oy	oi
em/pl**oy** des/tr**oy** r**oy**/al	t**oi**let dis/app/**oi**nt a/v**oi**d
con/v**oy**	app/**oi**nt/ment j**oi**nt cu/b**oi**d

Reading

Step 1

Say the word syllable by syllable.

Example: **em/ploy**

Step 2

Say the whole word.

Example: **employ**

Step 3

Say the **oy** sound.

oy

Step 4

Now trace the letter group for the **oy** sound on your finger.

Writing

Step 5

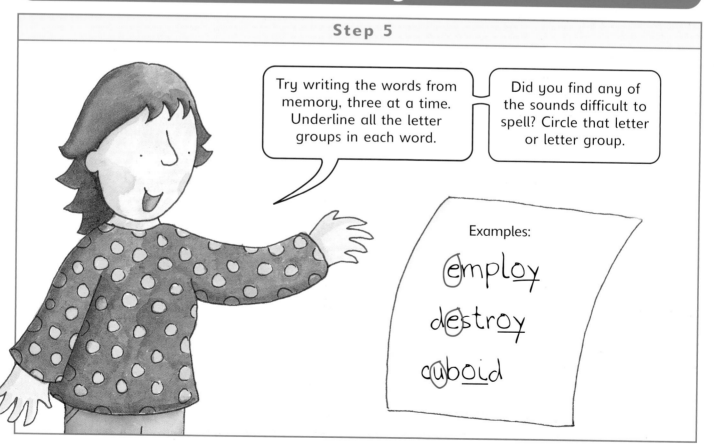

Try writing the words from memory, three at a time. Underline all the letter groups in each word.

Did you find any of the sounds difficult to spell? Circle that letter or letter group.

Examples:

employ

destroy

cuboid

Words containing *air*, *are*, *ear*, *ere* or *aer*

Before we start this page, let's look back at page 32 ...

Now let's look at some of those words – with endings added to them.

ing	ed	s	y ly	ier	iest
car**ing**	car**ed**	care**s**	hair**y**	hair**ier**	hair**iest**
star**ing**	star**ed**	chair**s**	rare**ly**		
shar**ing**	shar**ed**	bear**s**			

Reading

Step 1
Say the root word.
Example: **care**

Step 2
Say the word ending.
Example: **ing**

In words like **care**, the **e** is dropped before **ing** is added.

Here are some longer words which have the **air** sound in them.

In a few words, this vowel sound is spelled **aer**.

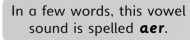
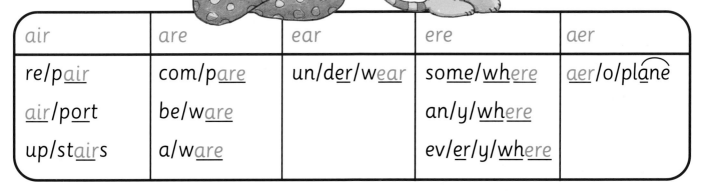

air	are	ear	ere	aer
re/p<u>air</u>	com/p<u>are</u>	un/der/w<u>ear</u>	some/<u>wh</u><u>ere</u>	<u>aer</u>/o/pl<u>a</u>ne
<u>air</u>/p<u>or</u>t	be/w<u>are</u>		an/y/<u>wh</u><u>ere</u>	
up/st<u>air</u>s	a/w<u>are</u>		ev/<u>er</u>/y/<u>wh</u><u>ere</u>	

54

Reading

Step 1

Say the word syllable by syllable.

Example: **re/pair**

Step 2

Say the whole word.

Example: **repair**

Step 3

Say the **air** sound.

air

Step 4

Now trace the letter group for the **air** sound on your finger.

Writing

Step 5

Try writing the words from memory, three at a time. Underline all the letter groups in each word.

Did you find any of the sounds difficult to spell? Circle that letter or letter group.

Examples:

bew<u>are</u>

<u>a</u>ny<u>wh</u>ere

s<u>o</u>m<u>e</u><u>wh</u>ere

Words containing or, aw, a, oor, al, ough, augh, oar or our

> Before we start this page, let's look back at page 33 ...

> Now let's look at some of those words – with endings added to them.

ing	ed	s	er	est
walk**ing**	walk**ed**	door**s**	poor**er**	poor**est**
talk**ing**	talk**ed**	horse**s**	tall**er**	tall**est**
crawl**ing**	crawl**ed**			

Reading

> The word ending **ed** can be pronounced **d**, **id** or **t**.

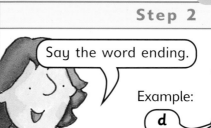

Step 1

> Say the root word.

Example: **walk**

Step 2

> Say the word ending.

Example: **d**

> Here are some longer words which have the **or** sound in them.

> In these words, this sound is spelled **ough**, **augh**, **oar** or **our**.

ough	augh	oar	our
b<u>ough</u>t	c<u>augh</u>t	b<u>oar</u>d	f<u>our</u>
br<u>ough</u>t	d<u>augh</u>/ter	cup/b<u>oar</u>d	p<u>our</u>
<u>th</u><u>ough</u>t	n<u>augh</u>/ty	s<u>oar</u>	c<u>our</u><u>se</u>

Reading

Step 1

Say the word syllable by syllable.

Example: **daugh/ter**

Step 2

Say the whole word.

Example: **daughter**

Step 3

Say the **augh** sound.

augh

Step 4

Now trace the letter group for the **augh** sound on your finger.

Writing

Step 5

Try writing the words from memory, three at a time. Underline all the letter groups in each word.

Did you find any of the sounds difficult to spell? Circle that letter or letter group.

Examples:

thought
cupboard
pour

Useful words

Word endings

The words in each of these sets follow a regular pattern and are easy to learn. Let your child practise learning and writing a set of words every day.

Words ending in *le*

Each of these words contains a short vowel followed by a double consonant.

middle	cuddle	giggle
apple	battle	kettle
little	puzzle	bubble
terrible	horrible	possible

Each of these words contains a short vowel followed by a two-consonant sound or two separate consonants.

simple	uncle	candle
handle	angle	triangle
rectangle	table	cable

Words ending in *en* or *on*

In each of these words, the final **en** or **on** is pronounced **un**.

garden	sudden	listen
open	spoken	taken
hidden	ridden	harden
apron	crayon	onion
dragon	lion	lesson
reason	season	button

Words ending in **tion**

In each of these words, the syllable **tion** is pronounced **shun**.

ac<u>tion</u>   a<u>ffection</u>   direc<u>tion</u>

infec<u>tion</u>   subtrac<u>tion</u>   rela<u>tion</u>

ope<u>ration</u>   celebra<u>tion</u>   educa<u>tion</u>

concentra<u>tion</u>   punctua<u>tion</u>   imagina<u>tion</u>

Words ending in **ous** or **ious**

In each of these words, the letters **ou** are pronounced **u**.

fam<u>ous</u>   n<u>e</u>rv<u>ous</u>   dang<u>erous</u>

en<u>or</u>m<u>ous</u>   gen<u>erous</u>   anxi<u>ous</u>

seri<u>ous</u>   f<u>urious</u>   c<u>urious</u>

Words ending in **ture**

nat<u>ure</u>   fut<u>ure</u>   mixt<u>ure</u>

pict<u>ure</u>   capt<u>ure</u>   advent<u>ure</u>

furnit<u>ure</u>   lit<u>er</u>at<u>ure</u>   temp<u>er</u>at<u>ure</u>

In each of these words, the syllable **ture** is pronounced **cher**.

Contractions

Contractions are words which have been shortened and put together. An apostrophe (') stands in for any missing letters.

Write each of these contractions as two complete words.

do not - don't

don't	couldn't	I'm	we're	we've	wasn't
can't	shouldn't	he's	you're	you've	weren't
	wouldn't	she's	they're	they've	

Now try these harder ones. You will have to write more than just a missing letter.

won't   shan't

Homophones

Homophones are words which sound the same but have different meanings and different spellings.

There are three things in my pocket.

It is their turn to play on the swings.

They're feeling happy today.

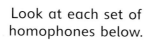

Look at each set of homophones below.

I'm going to put each word into a sentence, and say it aloud. Point to the correct word. Write the word.

to	our	for	sun	wood	great	past	flour
too	hour	four	son	would	grate	passed	flower
two		fore					
aloud	road	way	weather	where	patients	prints	bear
allowed	rode	weigh	whether	wear	patience	prince	bare
	rowed						
no	write	weak	hole	piece	coarse	new	wore
know	right	week	whole	peace	course	knew	war

Well done!

63

Superphonics

The simplest, fastest way to teach your child to read

Superphonics materials are available from all good bookshops. They can also be ordered with a credit card direct from the publisher by telephoning 01235 400414.

ISBN 0 340 77345 6 (pbk)
0 340 78768 6 (hbk)

ISBN 0 340 79567 0

ISBN 0 340 77346 4 ISBN 0 340 79568 9

ISBN 0 340 77347 2 ISBN 0 340 79569 7

ISBN 0 340 77348 0 ISBN 0 340 79570 0

ISBN 0 340 77349 9 ISBN 0 340 79571 9

ISBN 0 340 77354 5 ISBN 0 340 77350 2 ISBN 0 340 79573 5 ISBN 0 340 79894 7 ISBN 0 340 77352 9 ISBN 0 340 77351 0 ISBN 0 340 80550 1 ISBN 0 340 80549 8

ISBN 0 340 80545 5 ISBN 0 340 77353 7 ISBN 0 340 79703 7 ISBN 0 340 79893 9 ISBN 0 340 79896 3 ISBN 0 340 80546 3 ISBN 0 340 80551 X ISBN 0 340 79574 3

ISBN 0 340 80547 1 ISBN 0 340 79575 1 ISBN 0 340 79895 5 ISBN 0 340 80548 X

ISBN 0 340 79564 6 ISBN 0 340 79565 4 ISBN 0 340 80501 3 ISBN 0 340 79566 2 (pbk)
0 340 84170 2 (hbk)

Superphonics Spelling
ISBN 0 340 85195 3

Text copyright © 2002 Ruth Miskin
Illustrations copyright © 2002 James Wilkinson, Tim Archbold and Ella Burfoot
Editorial by Gill Munton
Design by Sarah Borny

First published in Great Britain 2002
10 9 8 7 6 5 4 3 2 1

First published in 2002 by Hodder Children's Books,
a division of Hodder Headline Limited,
338 Euston Road, London NW1 3BH

Printed in Hong Kong by Wing King Tong

A CIP record is registered by and held at the British Library.